Kissing the Shuttle

A Lyric History

Kissing the Shuttle

A Lyric History

Mary Ann Mayer

Blackstone River Books

Blackstone River Books
blackstoneriverbooks@gmail.com

ISBN: 978-0-692-06921-9

Poetry, Historical / Textile Mills, King Cotton, Early Industrialization / New England

Poetry, Historical / Tuberculosis, Open-Air Schools, Sanatoria / Rhode Island

History / Mill Conditions, Tuberculosis, Public Health / Rhode Island

First Edition

Front Cover Photo: "A moment's glimpse of the outer world…"
Library of Congress Prints and Photographs Division, Lewis Hines.

Rear Cover Photo: "Open-air schoolroom, Summit Street School, Pawtucket, 1910", Courtesy of Pawtucket Public Library Collection

I dedicate the poems to those who endured these work, living, and economic conditions, survived or didn't, and sometimes prospered. Although gone, your ordinary grace and sacrifices still matter, indeed, have imprinted upon us. You are the warp and weft of our living tapestry.

Most of all, in loving memory of
Dorothy (Walsh) Maitland & Robert Leo Maitland
for making sure I had all the tools I would need

Contents

Forward   ix
Introduction   3
A Note to the Reader   7

I.

Children Very Plenty   11
Mill Girl   14
Kissing the Shuttle   16
The Fresh Air School, 1908, Pawtucket, R.I.   18
Golden Rule   19
Jumping Lessons   22
The Superintendent Pins Up Positivity Posters   23
TB's Gifts   24
Taken Away to Wallum Lake Sanatorium   28
Occupational Therapy   29
Noon Whistle   30
White Water   33
Fever Dream   34
Children's Hall   35
Sanatorium Nursery   36
Class 3 Privileges   37
Gramma's House   40
Settling In   42
With Windows Open (health creeps in)   44
What Child Is This   45
Searchlight   48

II

The New Creed / Gospel of Industry	52
The Mill Bell & The Clothesline	54
The Super Pins Up More Positivity Posters	56
Charity Begins at Home	58
Woonsocket: America's Spunkiest City	61
World Heavyweight Champ Comes To Pawtucket	64
Coffle	68
The Work	70
Walt Whitman's Pants	72
Heavy Traffic	74
Ivory in Connecticut	75
Lords of The Loom, Lords of The Lash	80
Build Canals to Tame this Water...	82
Fresh Air Summer School, 1911 (*Don't Tread On Me*)	86
Sunday Afternoon	88
Aggie's Angel	90
Arrival Home	91
Afterword	93
Acknowledgments	97
Sources and Works Consulted	98
Image Source List	102
TB Progress Note	106
Author Note	108

Foreword

This book, by Mary Ann Mayer, opens with an insightful, informative, and moving introduction that illustrates the author's command of prose. Then it embarks on a lyrical tour of the industrialized Blackstone Valley and its tuberculosis sanatorium on Burrillville's Wallum Lake. The volume's unusual title "Kissing the Shuttle" was not an expression of love for the loom, but rather a method of refilling shuttles with bobbins of thread by placing one's lips against the shuttle's eye to pull its thread. Such a contagious practice, called "the kiss of death," infected the weavers, mainly women and young girls, thereby establishing a nexus between labor and debility—the Valley and the Lake.

That nexus is poignantly described in a litany of free verse, vivid and factually based, but embellished with poetic license. Historical illustrations and explanatory captions inform the story which, owing to the author's Valley roots, is a labor of love. This lyrical history also delves into the racial aspects of New England industry including its connection to slavery by affirming a connection between "the lords of the lash and the lords of the loom." Throughout, in a series of thirty-nine poems, Mayer skillfully weaves history with verse to create a tapestry of the Rhode Island textile industry that is a blend of both triumph and tragedy.

Patrick T. Conley
Historian Laureate of
Rhode Island

Kissing the Shuttle

A Lyric History

MILLS ON BLACKSTONE RIVER.

Mills on Blackstone River
Courtesy of Gail Conley

Introduction

Flowing fifty miles from Worcester, Massachusetts, to Pawtucket, Rhode Island, the Blackstone and its tributaries drain much of central New England's waters into Narragansett Bay and the sea. My poems are set in the Blackstone River Valley and its mill towns, "where the farmer met the machine and the immigrant discovered America," as stated by historian Steven Dunwell. Around 1800, for the first time in history, workers left the hardship and seasonal poverty of family farms to work in distant mills for hourly wages, participating in the "Rhode Island System of Manufacturing" and powering up the American Industrial Revolution. In 1788, nine out of ten citizens worked the land. After the War of 1812, it reversed; the majority worked in mills.

Through poetry, I explore the landscape of my ancestors and my youth. We follow the river where it leads, to discover and reenact the region's story . . . from the 1790s when spinning and weaving of cotton were mechanized, through the turn of the 20th century. How to conjure the experience of people whose contributions and suffering form the Blackstone River Valley's historical memory? I hope to show motifs of daily life during this radical shift to a mercantile society with its mass production of goods. Indeed, as persons created new machines, machines created a new person and way of life.

I found that interwoven with the story of the dominion of textile mills and the vigor, then decay, of mill towns, were other stories: Northern complicity in slavery to feed "Cotton Fever," the country's craving for finished cloth; the immigration wave and gain (and loss) of cultures; and how the smallest state led the nation in measures to curb and cure the tuberculosis epidemic. Municipal and World Health Organization records show that by 1905, tubuerculosis (TB) killed one in seven people in Europe and the Americas. In the Northeastern states, unsanitary, crowded mills, and housing created hotbeds of disease. In New York City that year, one-quarter of all recorded deaths were from TB. Immigrants were twice as likely to die of the disease. *Everyone* knew someone who had TB.

In Pawtucket, the birthplace of American manufacturing, bold reforms were underway, targeting workplace conditions (ventilation), practices (infection control), and child labor laws. By 1910, an estimated one-quarter of urban children were infected with tuberculosis. The co-founders of the Providence League for the Suppression of Tuberculosis, Dr. Ellen A. Stone and Dr. Mary S. Packard, launched the nation's first Fresh Air Schools—inspired by the Waldeschule (forest schools) in Germany. Frail children were given the opportunity for "open-air treatment" and schooling, instead of quarantine.

Initially proposed to educate ten students in renovated horse sheds at the Friends Meeting House in Providence, one began in what is now the Providence Preservation Society on Meeting Street, another in downtown Pawtucket near Slater's Mill. Public school practices a nation now takes for granted, got their start in these Fresh Air Schools. The model quickly spread through the country, establishing, among other things, the first school hot lunch program and outdoor recess! Its motto: *Double rations of air, double rations of food, half-rations of work.* By the early 1920s there were similar schools in over 150 American cities.

Several poems are set in the Rhode Island schools. Others follow a resilient child named Aggie through her day in the state sanatorium, commonly known as Wallum Lake. It was both a self-sufficient farm and "contagion hospital." Aggie and her relations are a composite of my ancestors who emigrated from England, Ireland, Scotland, and Quebec—most worked in the mills and lived in their shadow. My Irish grandmother lost three newborns in four years, before being suddenly widowed with three more. I never met those grandparents, but knew the sadness and stoicism passed down.

Those I *did* know, on my mother's side, came from England and Quebec, met in the mill, crossing social and religious lines to marry. In 1914, as a teenage apprentice, Pop-Pop "worked his way up," later moving his young family into the "Superintendent's House." He spent his life at the mill, retiring in 1970. (Allegiance to mill and machine was as common as his missing three fingers at the knuckles).

As a whole, I trust that the poems recall life in "the Valley"— the roar of the falls beside Slater's red mill; in the "many-tongued neighborhoods," stairwells of triple-deckers filled with "chemistries of onion, cabbage, turnip," and downtown Pawtucket "newly strung with telephone lines." I feel kinship with that spirit of working hard to create things to build a life. Labor is our heritage and idealism is in our DNA. To those builders and progressive reformers, I say: We will continue your work to improve "us"—our collective vitality and future.

M.A.M.

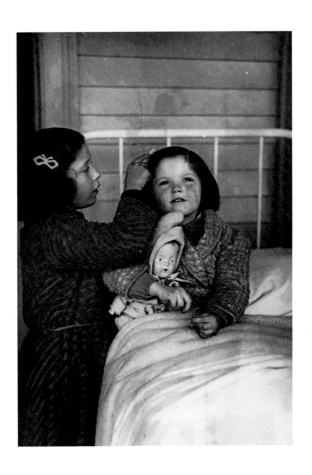

A Note to the Reader

Kissing the Shuttle is loosely chronological except for Aggie's "story," which is meant to be read as a sequence, from "TB's Gifts" through the end of Section One. An imagined character, her calm demeanor may seem to belie the distress of a child who is institutionalized. Yet at the risk of depicting the sanatorium experience through rose-colored glasses, one-dimensionally, or "sanitizing" this dread disease, I wanted Aggie to thrive. Writing in her voice cheered me, as did reading numerous first-hand accounts from this period. To my surprise, these suggest a not unpleasant life—ample society, pastimes, fresh food and air, healthful regimes—especially in the early years of these sanatoria. Attractively advertised as "health-centres" in popular magazines, resort towns such as Sun City, AZ, Saranac Lake, NY, and Colorado Springs, grew from the influx of "rest-cure seekers," who later settled in those areas. Although I didn't study it, I imagine that, over the decades, with new immigration, war, the epidemic's peak, then the Depression, public funds dwindled and distinctions grew between private and state facilities (respectively serving rich or the working poor) that were significant, and in some situations, drastic.

Pawtucket Falls and the Blackstone River

I

History is the function of any one of us
Charles Olsen

Erosion, a great builder of landscapes
Diane Ackerman

A moment's glimpse of the outer world

Spinners and doffers

Children Very Plenty

Mills rise on New England bedrock,
on riverbanks in steep-sided valleys,
alongside falls and fast-moving streams.

A good place for manufactories!
Ideally a toll-road or waterway
links factory to port.

Ideally,
"A place very disagreeably suited.
The inhabitants poor, their homes in decline,
and children appearing very plenty . . . widows and children . . ."

Writes Obidiah Brown in 1797,
to William Almy in Providence,
of the good place he'd found for their manufactory.

❧ The "Rhode Island System of Labor" relied upon family groups.
By 1830, 55% of the mill workers in R.I. were children. Historical
records mention children as young as seven in the work force. Even in
1910, only 48% of children attended school; truancy laws were poorly
enforced.

A young spooler

Sadie Pfeifer, 48 inches tall . . .

Barefoot on cotton mule

Carder breathing in cotton

Mill Girl

Sun glinting off a wooden loom.
The clanking of chains,
the clack of the flying shuttle
through the shed,
the warp and weft,
the in and out,
the whir and throstle
of looms and spinners
from first to last slant light
across the fifteen-hour day.

The cleaning, combing, carding of cotton,
the spinning of thread,
the rustle of cloth,
the mill girl, her tongue
rolled tight against her upper lip
to keep out sweat-salt,
cotton lint,
a fleck in the corner
of her mouth.

Her neck is wet and aches
as she arches,
stretches her body across
the wooden frame
to weight the loom,
to tension the threads,
she strokes the warp
combed to a sheen
as if riding a horse,
as if one with the beast,
neck lengthening
across an uncrossable field.

Girls at weaving machine . . .

Kissing the Shuttle

The toll it took,
to spin the thread
to weave the cloth
that spewed the lint
that choked the lungs
that made the young weavers,
women and girls,
most susceptible
to illnesses that would fell them,
white lung, brown lung,
TB, influenza, contagions they spread

Weaving cotton, the air had to be moist.
Windows closed tight, floors kept wet,
pipes overhead sprayed the air,
"steaming" the cotton and the girls
each tending four looms,
refilling shuttles
with fresh bobbins of thread
by "kissing the shuttle"—
lips pressed against the shuttle's eye
then sharply inhaling
to pull the thread through,

sucking lint and toxins into their lungs
three hundred times a day!
They'd share the shuttles,
reuse the shuttles,
kiss the shuttles,
mouths thick with the taste
of what lodged in their lungs:
lint, fibers, dirt, a glue called "size"
and chemicals if the thread was dyed.

They'd cough the dirt up and start again
and not only that—
these girls with ruined lungs coughing up cotton,
lips bruised, teeth coming loose,
were just *girls*
so, they'd share lipstick, reapply it
after all that kissing
left behind
in the weaving room.

Young woman "kissing the shuttle," called "the kiss of death"

❧ Weavers had the highest TB rate of all mill workers. The act of 'kissing the shuttle,' using the mouth to pull thread through the eye, led to the spread of disease. Dr. Charles Chapin, Health Officer for RI, was the first to connect TB with mill conditions and practices, leading the campaign for reforms. In 1911, Massachusetts was the first state to ban the suction (kissing) shuttle, mandating self-threading ones.

The Fresh Air School, 1908, Pawtucket, R.I.

Out of congested tenements they come, anemic
underweight, frail ones, tubercular
in the early, sapping stage before the lesions—
not to sanatorium but to school!

The first hot school lunch in the land,
a schoolyard romp every twenty minutes—
air as cure, air as elixir
for lungs unused to the appetite for it.

For twenty children,
once thought beyond aid or learning,
the sense of belonging
is as warm as the soup they sip
this morning, between art and first recess,

schooled into a generous life,
a happy picture.

In the first decade of the twentieth century, an estimated one-quarter of urban children were infected with TB. R.I. doctors Ellen A. Stone and Mary S. Packard opened the nation's first two Fresh Air schools. The model quickly spread through the country with its motto: "Double rations of air, double rations of food, half-rations of work."

Golden Rule

Double rations of air, double rations of food, half-rations of work.
Tall windows with muslin screens open wide
to autumn sleet; on a pot-bellied stove,
mittens and bright paintings dry.

Twenty pupils, bundled up, sit inside
their Eskimo bag—warm
drawstring sack, little woolen helmet,
a hot stone for their feet beneath each desk.

They breathe their lessons in
and the world offers itself—spiral
of scrubbed blue days, moving clouds and
changing light, sheets of rain swishing in on the wind.

Roar of the falls, Slater's red mill, gust
and whir of the water wheel, ever-revolving,
churning mist and rainbows—
explorers on the verge,

learning wilderness skills
at every turn.

Open-air schoolroom at the Summit Street School in Pawtucket,
c. 1910

Open-air classroom at Slater Jr. High School, c. 1920

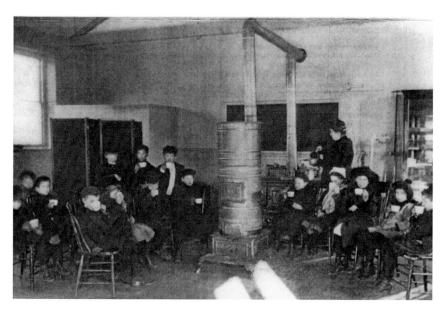

Pupils at Meeting Street School were served hot meals
mid-morning and at noon

Jumping Lessons

Science in the sparrow nest on the sill,
loose cup of twigs woven with grass and
web; inside, lined with scraps of wool
and the egg sacs of jumping spiders.

Laughing gulls overhead; below,
thump, thump of Double Dutch;
jumpers run through
the swinging loops, turners chant

Cinderella, dressed in yellow
Went upstairs to kiss a 'fella
Made a mistake and kissed a snake
How many doctors did it take?

Faster, faster . . .
All in together girls
It's fine weather girls
When is your birthday?
Please jump in!
January, February, March, April, May . . .

1,2,3,4,5,6,7,8
All out other girls
It's fine weather girls
When is your birthday?
Please jump out!

The Superintendent Pins Up Positivity Posters

Positivity Poster # 1 (Beside the Time-clock)

New Scientific Discovery!
Germs spread disease!
Gents, rid yourself of beard-germs. Shave your whiskers!
Ladies, raise your skirt hems out of the dirt!
Let's defeat germs!

Positivity Poster # 8 (Weaving Room)

Before another man is lost
Before another child sickens
Our factory will do its part
And together we'll make a difference!

Positivity Poster # 3 (Lunch Room)

Dirt and germs
Are the bosom friends of sickness
Let's show them the door!

Positivity Poster #32 (Ladies' Dormitory)

The American Red Cross says:
Try "Kleenex"!
Ladies, fold your handkerchiefs away
"Kleenex" is cleaner, tidier . . .
Your first defense!

TB's Gifts

Shorter skirts
Better razors
Hot school lunch and formal recess
Kleenex (Never, ever wipe your nose on your sleeve)
Christmas Seals
Positivity Posters in the workplace
Labor laws & shorter hours
Anti-spitting laws
Public health campaigns & Dixie cups
Training for all in the proper way of brushing teeth—
and for children, how to live as orphans in other people's houses

Wallum Lake Sanatorium image
Courtesy of G. Wayne Miller

꙳ TB is caused by exposure to tubercle bacilli bacteria, in infected
sputum or other expectorants. There is often a six month incubation
period before symptoms appear. Another possible cause, especially among
infants and children, was consuming contaminated milk. Rhode Island
adopted a law requiring that each county have a commissioner to
investigate animals thought to be infected, and quarantine these animals
for examination. In 1920 it was noted that five of seven samples of "baby's
milk" collected in Providence were contaminated with tubercle bacilli and
that not more than 60 per cent of the Providence milk supply was
pasteurized. (RIHS, P. Griswold)

By 1938, TB was under control in some states, thanks to cleaner water supplies and improved health care. Sanatoriums began to admit healthier children with bronchial conditions and juvenile arthritis. A major turning point came in 1943, when the antibiotic streptomycin was shown to arrest advanced TB, although it was not widely used until after 1950.

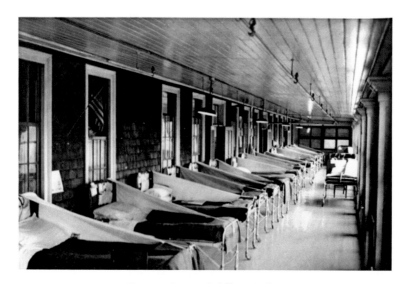

Sanatorium at Wallum Lake

The State Sanatorium for Tuberculosis, on Wallum Lake in the state's northwestern corner, offered open-air treatment and was also a self-sufficient 250 acre farm. When it opened in 1905, TB was the leading cause of death in R.I. Wallum Lake took in more than 10,000 patients between 1905-1930. Later named the Zambarano Unit of The Eleanor Slater Hospital after one of the facility's noted physicians, its last TB ward closed in 1982. Until the widespread use of antibiotics, half of those infected died within five years. In 1954, 16,000 died compared to 120,000 (nationwide) at its peak in 1918. "White Plague" or "Consumption" was the common inheritance of rich and poor alike. Strengthening the body's defenses against the bacillus through diet (a glass of milk every four hours!), controlled rest and exercise, fresh air and sunlight, was thought to be curative in the early 1900's. Patients often slept outdoors year-round.

Taken Away to Wallum Lake Sanatorium

Spring snow fell all night
drifts for the kids to play in
a kitchen door slams

laughter, *clomp clomp*
of boots overhead, then down the back stairs

Mum stares out the window, weeping
Gramma brushes and buttons my wool coat
presses Daddy's handkerchief into my palm

Doctor Gaudet says I'll be alright
No harm will come, the cure will take

Father Roque nods, his hand on my head
in blessing, promises
I can listen to prayers on the radio

A knock on the door
Kids yell, *Aggie, ya comin? there's a snowball fight!*

No one answers. The room falls quiet
while President Wilson reassures
the nation

Occupational Therapy

At first, Aggie draws scary stands of trees,
scraggly pines on the edge of woods.
She's warned, don't cry, never ask
When will I . . . ? Who died? Who'll make it out?

24 hour rest with bedpan: Class 1
Bathroom privileges only: Class 2
can "dangle" legs five times a day,
sit on the edge of the bed and swing them.

When will I . . . ? (Don't ask)
Who died?
Who'll make it out? Who ran away? (Not you)
Can I go back to school?

She weaves potholders on a finger loom,
reads Clara Barton and Brothers Grimm classics,
waits for the cart to be wheeled between rooms,
accepts charcoal, crayons, white canvas.

Consumptives must spend all day reclined
side-by-side, in rooms or out on the veranda.
Coloring, Aggie stays within the lines,
careful not to cross over.

Noon Whistle

The men eat meat pies beneath the elms,
smile and wave to Ellen walking by.
One whispers, "She'll marry again, with twins to feed."

They miss Joseph and notice
his widow's hemline rising, as she climbs
the hill to the Fresh Air School
and her new job as girls' lavatory matron.

Her husband, their friend, three months dead
of consumption, then newborns. Her eight year old,
Aggie, sweet kid, in the "San" too— caught
a cold that flew to her lungs, got infected
caring for her daddy.

The mill families
and parish will give what they can,
send prayers her way and Bingo money;

When Joseph passed, the priest brought the news
and still visits every week for comfort.
He was helping Aggie prepare for her First Communion,
God willing, she's out by June.

69 TAKE FRIEDMANN CURE
The Washington Post (1877-1954); Apr 10, 1913; ProQuest Historical Newspapers The Washingt
pg. 3

69 TAKE FRIEDMANN CURE

Patients at Rhode Island Sanitarium Treated With Vaccine.

St. Louis Doctor Seeks Injunction Against Sale of Rights, Claiming Prior Contract.

Providence. R. I., April 9.—Before a gathering of the medical profession of the State Dr. Friedrich F. Friedmann today injected the vaccine which he claims is a cure for tuberculosis into 69 of the 124 patients at the Wallum Lake Sanitarium. a State institution.

For five hours Dr. Friedmann interviewed and treated patients. He selected 76 men and women representing all stages of the disease. but seven of these were not treated because he had to depart to keep an appointment in this city. He promised Dr. Harry Lee Barnes. the superintendent of the sanitarium, that he would return there before he leaves Rhode Island.

Tomorrow he will treat private patients for fees for the first time in this country.

St. Louis. April 9.—Dr. Albert Von Hoffman. of St. Louis. today directed his attorney in New York to apply for an injunction to restrain Dr. Friedmann from closing a contract with any one for the disposition of his tuberculosis vaccine in case Dr. Friedmann should attempt to put his remedy on the market.

Dr. Von Hoffman claims to have a prior contract with Dr. Friedmann for the commercial rights to the vaccine. and today gave out the alleged contract. This is dated October 24, 1912, and provides for a payment of $1,000,000 to Dr. Friedmann.

31

AGAINST FRIEDMANN CURE.

Dr Barnes of Rhode Island Sanatorium Reports 17 Percent of Cases Treated Are Worse.

PROVIDENCE, Sept 4—In a preliminary report to the Rhode Island Medical Society today, Dr Harry Lee Barnes, superintendent of the State Sanatorium at Wallum Lake, declared that the 120 sufferers from pulmonary tuberculosis treated by Dr Friedmann last April with his turtle vaccine "have shown none of the immediate and wonderful results reported by Friedmann and others before the Berlin Medical Society."

"On the contrary," Dr Barnes added, "about 17 percent of the cases have shown an increased activity of the disease, which would not have been expected under ordinary sanatorium treatment."

Dr Barnes reported one patient with joint tuberculosis had shown marked improvement.

A number of doctors, among them Dr W. G. Dwinell and Dr T. J. Smith, came to the defense of the German bacteriologist. Dr Dwinell said: "It is not enough to line up a lot of patients in the dining room and ask them how they feel. I can point to as many successes among the patients as he can failures."

Experimental "turtle vaccine" injections by a visiting German doctor led to two patient deaths in July, 1913.

White Water

She waits for the door
to open, to see
what was not spoken of,
hear the voice
of the one
who now is gone.
Her father's voice
swirls around her, white
water whispering,
"Please don't close the door"

Fever Dream

Chorus of coughing, coughing, coughing.
Three rows down, feverish moaning
So sorry so sorry. A boy cries out
Am I dying?

Nurses flock to children, face down
floating. Dark sludge rising—
nurses bale with rag pails
unraveling— bobbing heads, leaden eyes

one-by-one
they turn aside, grow
black feathers,
mutter spells, swoop
down, smothering each child.

Aggie screams dark-red (or is it
her heart pounding?) wakes, fighting
her sheets, drenched and knotted . . .
flings off the weight, smells the rush of rain
her heat, her sweat salt.

A brush pulled through her hair,
a body taking shape beside her . . .
Nurse Bea smiles,
Fever's broke, Aggie; It's a GOOD morning!
kisses Aggie's brow, her rag doll too,

props the pillow, sets the breakfast tray down,
shoos a bee away,
tells the same joke every morning;
I'm a Bea but I don't sting!

Laughing, leaves Aggie
to her sunny yolk, mug of milk,
her rag doll watching,
one shoe-button eye still chipped,
a smile that hasn't dropped a stitch.

Children's Hall

A table in the corner, set for one
Pineapple-upside-down cake
The special sweet for a child leaving
One balloon floats up, taps the ceiling

Sanatorium Nursery

The tiny rock sparrow is equipped with
a tongue toughened with a stiff skeletal structure
and horny palate, which works like a mini-nutcracker
to crush seeds and feed its young

Nurses push carts of ruffled cups
through rows of creaky cribs.
They tend the nests
with overhanging limbs and ministrations,

bestow on each, a kiss
redolent of ivory soap
and licorice.
Checking breath, saliva, fever graphs,

they pass between rows.
Out the window
a light quilt of snow
on colonial gravestones

The golden tanager builds nests in protected sites
a woodpecker's hole
an abandoned oriole nest
even a scavenged honeycomb

Class 3 Privileges

Fever gone and lesion-free, doing well
without medicine to keep her pulse down

Aggie advances to Class 3
light occupation and walks on-grounds

She's gathering strength; things are looking up
Come June, her grandmother will take her home

in time to make her First Communion!
For now, she enjoys

Sunday visits to the hennery
the milking shed, the plow horse in his field

the dank scent of the piggery
when the wind blows just right

She likes things sealed in
so caps jelly jars with paraffin

puts things in place
like pickled beans on the shelf

spools the clothesline
out and in, straightens the pins

helps the milk-man unload his wagon
taking care the bottles don't jiggle

and unclots
the cream solid on the top

helps the cook
for special celebrations

turn pineapple upside-down cakes
right-side up

Idella Almon (with hat) ... ... his horse and buggy ride in

1916, Idella Almon (in hat), one of three patients enjoying a buggy ride.
(below)1917, handwritten "X" on photo marks Idella's absence
from the variety show. She'd died.

Wallum Lake Frolics A Success

Wallum Lake, R. I.—A gala and tremendously successful New Year Frolics of 1941 was staged in the beautifully pine green decorated Auditorium of the Wallum Lake House last Thursday evening, presented by the patients of the Wallum Lake Sanatorium, under the general chairmanship of Marion L. Murray, hard-working Social Worker, and a corps of equally-well-deserving assistants. The program was directed by Vera Farrari.

The Auditorium, arranged in cabaret fashion, was filled to its capacity, and patients in wards were given a treat by hearing the proceedings via loud speaker system. Close to 400 filled the Auditorium.

As a prelude to the program, all entertainers paraded through the wards starting at 6:30 p. m., heralded by a triumvirate of instrumentalists, including, James Holland, and Vito Graneiri, drums, and Joseph Petrucci, clarinet.

Wallum Lake Frolics

(Continued from Page 1)

bartender, replete with handle bar moustachio, was voted wearing the funniest get-up, and subsequently acquired a necktie, donated by the Berk Shoe Store. John Carney won the door prize donated by the New York Store. Mary Sullivan received a compact as Hairless Joe.

A novel table decoration was candlelight service wherein an apple served as a base for wax uprights.

Festivity reigned, aided and abetted by various town groups who gave of their paraphernalia. Bridge tables were loaned by the American Legion Post, and St. Theresa's Church, both of Harrisville, and the Pawtucket Lodge of the Benevolent and Protective Order of Elks. The Pawtucket Lodge of Elks also donated $25.00, which was used to purchase noisemakers, mardi gras hats, snap favors, and other items.

The General Program F____

1. Song, "Old Gang Of Mine", Robert Lawson, John Ladefan.

2. Skit, "Dog Patch Revue"— Li'l Abner, Thomas Caples; Daisy Mae, Mary McKenna; Pansy Yokum, Louis Keefe; Lucifer Yokum, Gretchen Parker; Fruitful, Francis Kelly; Frightful, William Andrea; Mitzi Mudlark, Jean Lutz; Hairless Joe, Mary Sullivan; Black Rufe, Charles Dyer; Marry'n Sam, Nicholas Taccone; Mrs. Fantasia Brown, William Clark; Sadie Hawkins, Vera Ferrari.

3. Song, "Does Your Heart Beat For Me", Lucy Perry, Elizabeth Rickson, Gretchen Parker.

Gramma's House

I can't go back home yet,
although I'm well again.

Mum has the twins to care for, worries
our tenement is overcrowded

and fever germs might get me.
So Gramma took me in.

At first, her Minny Mouse shoes scare me,
her ticking clocks

the bookcase, so white, so quiet
the dust on blue silk flowers.

I feel like an elephant in a china shop
visiting poodles made of glass.

I'm not ready for school
but will be soon, the man says

who comes to check my fever graph and spit.
So I stay home and color (Mum's voice in my head)

Don't run, don't laugh; if you cough
they'll put you back in again

Twice a week Mum visits after work;
she's sad, so I try not to cry or be scolded

for acting like the child
I don't feel like at all.

She hugs me hard, says
I'm helping her and my twin sisters too,

by staying here awhile.
I'm getting to know each window and every latch,

the way the crocheted curtains sway
and cast their lacy shadows on the floor,

the arrangement of bone china in the hutch,
which teacups have chips

and how to place them out of view (when company comes).
One is mine, paper-thin but strong!

and how long the kettle purrs
before it sings, louder, louder, louder, and I can pour.

Settling In

I take a good look around Gramma's house,
not the way orphans do, or immigrants
who wake in a bed not their own
with different flavors in their mouths,

but as me, Aggie (not Agatha in "the San" anymore).
Here, the walls are alive with pictures of those
who love and look like me, although we haven't met.
Ancestors are rooting for me!

My grandfather, Pop-Pop's, room is mine.
Cherry tobacco in the bureau drawer, his Meerschaum pipe,
its chewed mouthpiece hasn't felt lips in years,
in mine, tastes burnt and sweet.

Gramma stayed here when she was sad
(before I came). Now, on Saturdays
I sweep dust bunnies out
of the living room corners

and visit the milk-glass poodle and dachshunds
on the tea-tables beside the winter chairs.
Gramma wants me to name each one
and fill their hollow backs with peppermints

while she Pine-Sols the loor.
As it dries, we walk outside to find
the first wild raspberries,
the brambles humming with horseflies.

Gramma and her friend make pies for Sunday.
Pastry rounds rolled out after supper,
the rolling pin, white with flour, resting;
they share a schooner of beer mixed with lemonade.

Drowsy in the bath, feeling loved, because
through the door Gramma tells me to sing
so she can be sure I didn't drown.

Speaking Quebecois real fast
with her friend, I hear words I'd know anywhere—
smart girl, my lamb chop, vivante, she go soon
école école école!

With Windows Open (health creeps in)

Science in the gathering clouds breaking open,
geography in the river's map to the sea,
geometry in V-formation flying south on steady wings

Scrubbed blue days, moving clouds
and changing light, sheets of rain
swishing in on the wind

Music in the yacking gulls
and schoolyard chatter—
lungs yielding to laughter, limbs unused to running,
turning supple, elastic

Boys play tag, leap-frog, and "conkers"—
horse chestnut on a string swung against another's
(the one that doesn't break, crowned King)
Girls skip rope with fancy footwork
        "calling in" each girl by name, *Ellen, Dottie, Laura*

Skipping faster, faster, turners chant:
Judy and Randy sittin' in a tree
K-I-S-S-I-N-G
First comes love, then comes marriage
then comes Judy with a baby carriage

What Child Is This?

Aggie's lost in her work, wearing
her white sailor shirt
just last week, gift-wrapped
under the tree
she un-dresses today,
ritual of green surrender.

She unhooks
fragile ornaments
the needles have grown fond of,
coaxes them from dance-floor of branch and bough,
returns the dazzle to cardboard boxes.
First, she holds each up to the light
for its secret meaning to shine through,
cup her reflection, spin the room.

The tree, browning, dismasted
of its silver star
still nurses its sugar water
with the thirst of
the near-abandoned.
Is it ready, or not ready, to be taken?
The house is still.
Then a knock at the door, someone
knocking harder and harder then bearing down
on the bell—

Aggie freezes, peeks through
the drapes, sees the mean girl on the stoop,
pig-tailed; behind her, icicles glisten like tusks.
She wants Aggie to play with, listen to her
songs about kids from the "San,"
hunt Fool's Gold, black things in snow,
the residue of meteorites that killed the dinosaurs.

At first, the school nurse made her play with Aggie
who hoped they'd feel affection soon,
So all fall, they were cowgirls with cap-guns, rode
broom-stick ponies, made mud-pies, jumped puddles,
hid in the doghouse, swung from the tree.
Aggie grew tall and fast, became the one winning races.
Then it got rough—

when she didn't want to play "doctor" anymore—
always the patient,
undershirt pulled up, poked in the stomach,
on her back, squirming,
those greasy pig tails brushing her face.
Once, she heard a boy laugh . . .

Today, Gramma's gone out. The girl gets in—
grabs fistfuls of straw from the manger, kicks
the silent figurines, stomps on nests of ribbons
and garland set aside for next year, taunting Aggie
See? Your ugly empty tree. STUPID TB tree. Donner & Blitzen pooped
on your roof! Santa left you lumps of coal cuz the black inside you
makes you not right!

The girl is imploding. Turning invisible, her dark side,
her instinct to break things.
Something in Aggie is awakening.
The tree burns and glows from within
its radial heart, rings of wisdom;
not making a sound,
rising against the wall.

The room leans in to listen.
Outside, it starts to snow,
trees kneel down in lazy halleluiahs.
What child is this?
It can be told no other way—
The child of whom we now can sing.

Searchlight

When the floorboards creak
and the quiet chimes in
like clockwork
Aggie slips

into her dream
at Wallum Lake
alone, retracing steps
trawling strange, waxed floors

searching
to the edge
of a moonlit lawn—
white shine upon her nightdress

white hollyhocks nod
to the air and a path leads through
a garden gate, ajar
to a fine old house beyond

She tries to read the mood of the house
counts the panes while the lights are out
She mustn't fall asleep
no, it's almost time

Aren't her mother and sisters there
in broken moonlight
behind the high window, white
with mullions?

She waits a little longer
lets her ancestors snore in their sepia hall
The house will wake untroubled
and welcome her in

II

TIME TABLE

of the

Whittenton Manufacturing Co.

The hours of Labor on all days, except Saturdays, will be from 6 1-2 o'clock A. M. until 6 1-2 P. M., and on Saturdays from 6 1-2 A. M. to 4 P. M.

DINNER, 35 MINUTES.

MORNING BELLS.

First Bell will ring at	. . . . .	5 A. M.
Second " "	. . . . .	6 "
Third " "	. . . . .	6.25 "

DINNER BELLS.

Ring out, ...	at 12 M.
Ring in, ...	at 12.30 P. M.

EVENING BELLS.

Ring out at 6 1-2 P. M., except on Saturdays.
On Saturdays, the bell will ring out at 4 P. M.

YARD GATE

Will be closed exactly at 6.30 A. M. and 12.35 P. M.

The overseers and second hands, will be in their rooms at the first stroke of the ringing in bells.

The engine or water-wheel will start at first stroke of the ringing in bells.

Taunton, Sept. 5th, 1865.

New World, Old World Bells, 1865

50

City of Pawtucket Flag, adopted in 1974.
It shows the old Slater Mill, its dam, and the tail race.

Punching time cards in a time clock around 1920

The New Creed

. . . Who has seen a cotton plant? There is something of this material which adapts itself in a peculiar degree to the application of machines . . . (Alexander Hamilton, 1790)

The Mill: America's First Church
Serves America's First God: The Machine

Replace the scythe and patient farming rhythms
Din of a thousand braid machines and spinning jennys

Automate $$ that ancient human need to clothe and decorate . . .

1910 Industrial Discipline
This work demands a clock: *Tick Tock:*
Time: Cards, Time Clock, Time-Study Men
In labcoats with clipboards and stop watches

Strict behavioral control for irresponsible, ignorant laborers

"Labor Multipliers"
"Stretch-outs"—more machines assigned each worker
"Light-up time"— five o'clock in the evening signaling
two hours more work
"Speed-ups"—Machines cranked to the highest speed
Labor "paced" for the first time in human history for constant
production:

Maximum production per worker = the highest degree of civilization

Gospel of Industry = Efficiency

Hail High-Priest and King: Frederick Winslow Taylor

Mercantiles $ Metronomes $ Humans $ Motion systems
They are not one, two, ten $ Make a system of them.
Each one makes a greater sum

Machines yoked together, suspended from chains

To and fro swings the   burning metal censer
incense smoke swirls   the vestibule, the vaulting,
the steeple,   the old bell ringing in the old way . . .

Unto us over us the night sky voices heavenward rise . . .

*"Let our prayers be set before You as incense, the lifting up
of hands as the evening sacriice . . ."*

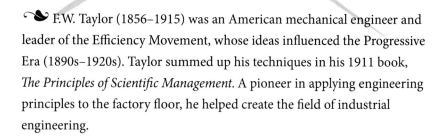

   F.W. Taylor (1856–1915) was an American mechanical engineer and
leader of the Efficiency Movement, whose ideas influenced the Progressive
Era (1890s–1920s). Taylor summed up his techniques in his 1911 book,
The Principles of Scientific Management. A pioneer in applying engineering
principles to the factory floor, he helped create the field of industrial
engineering.

The Mill Bell & The Clothesline

No one out of earshot or reach.
No matter how bone-tired, how deep asleep,
In the dark, all wake, summoned
by the bell that patterns the lives that swing between

its call on Monday and the end of the Saturday shift . . .
to make the cloth, the calico.
No one out of earshot or reach
of its long, slow clang—
oooo--calic-o- calic-o- calic-oooo

No matter how bone-tired, how deep asleep,
inside the rain-gray triple-deckers,
all wake to the bell
that echoes

the country's craving for cloth.
Hungry for calico!—
the latest patterns, the prettiest, the best,
from Pawtucket and Central Falls.

All the three-deckers, built to last,
house workers flooding in—
to a hungry country,
its many-tongued neighborhoods
and old world smells . . .

meat pies heavily cloved to disguise
what may have spoiled inside;
cook-sweat clings to horse-hair plaster walls,
chemistry of onion, cabbage, turnip

fills stair-wells, wafts
onto tenement porches,
where clotheslines criss-cross
sagging with shirts that never dry

the same blue shirts
that cling, damp,
to the backs of the laborers,
a gray-blue blue-gray line reaching to dawn.

The Super Pins Up More Positivity Posters

Positivity Poster # 23 (Above the Time Clock)

Let's work together
to fight the spread of TB
Practice hygiene
All washrooms now have
new bars of soap
and foot powder

Positivity Poster # 38 (In the Carding/Combing Room)

Germs cause sickness
When you spread a germ
Someone else
Suffers for it
Someone else has to
Work harder
Do your job
Don't spread germs

Positivity Poster #60 (On Every Bulletin Board)

TB is Contagious!
We will fight Germs with Enthusiasm
Remember, POSITIVITY is Contagious
Be enthusiastic
Stay POSITIVE!

IMPORTANT ANNOUNCEMENT!
COMPANY PICNIC, JUNE 30th
Sayles Bleachery Field, Lincoln

Come say hello to the Red Cross
after you've had
your fill of
ham and beans,
strawberry shortcake
and softball

"Gimme one - me sister's got it."

1907, the first Christmas Seal
campaign to stamp out TB.

Charity Begins at Home

as told by my dad, Bob Maitland, who pedaled "The Times" as a boy

my throw'n arm was good
so the *Pawtucket Times* kept me on
delivering before school
I'd throw each newspaper
from my bicycle
up on to every porch on Sweet
and half of Suffolk
my aim
was so good
I never even braked or got off my bike
to run up the steps
or fish one out of the shrubs
I was the only paperboy
on the Darlington route
some customers tipped two cents a week
I had four blocks of jickies, polaks,
frenchies and micks
and I had to be nice to all of em
      Mum made sure I knew
she'd hear about it if I wasn't
she wouldn't let me charge
certain ones if they were having hard times
made me pay for their paper outta my tips
so when Mrs. Boba stopped the paper
after her husband died
I still pedaled by her house   slow
just in case she changed her mind
because even if you're sad
so long as you're alive
news is good
right?

Noon Hour. Group of Workers at American Yarn Mfg., Pawtucket, R.I.

St. Jean Baptiste Day Parade, June 24th, 1906, Pawtucket, R.I.

Illustration of a shoeshine boy and a paper boy was the letterhead for the
Pawtucket Boys Club (now Pawtucket Boys and Girls Club), c.1905

Woonsocket: America's Spunkiest City

". . . In the floating world, may you discover grace."—Galway Kinnell

My great-aunts, ancient, hang their wash on the line and swear
(again), it was the hand of God that closed the mills
that November day, in the morning, when the light
never touched ground, but spread an eerie glow.

I sit cross-legged on the ground, handing them up clothespins
and hear again, how that day the bell gonged at 6 am
and out of the tenements streamed the "helps"
following the call to work . . .
That is, all but the cautious few,

who read into the pre-dawn light
a premonition—a warning,
not to leave their young at home alone . . .
although many did go, to tend
their sleepless machines . . .

Who could foresee the danger about to descend?

By noon, the screaming, howling wind of a nameless
Nor'easter spinning its long arms of rain,
shatters panes, drowns out every other sound,
floor-trembling, rumbling more thunderous than
a thousand braid machines and spinning frames—
as those at their stations listen, tremble, pray.

Some still swear it was the hand of God that closed the mills.
My aunts say, "the whole valley drowned"
(making the sign of the cross) as if it were a biblical event,
that morning the light didn't touch ground
and the sky, blood-red, summoned the rivers to rise

and *"dams to burst asunder and release upon the valleys through which
they ran more terrible torrents than the inhabitants had ever seen."*

Their laundry starched and hung, just a few hankies left,
my aunts rest, nod their heads
and recall for each other (again) how the water rose
through the floorboards, up to the sills—
and they, with other kids, climbed on tables and chairs
to wait for rescue, not knowing what else to do.

They tell the story of Monsignor
in the street, saying his own confession,
praying with others in glottal languages
for deliverance from the terrible torrent, the hellish scene—

pale arms and legs swept over the falls, disappearing
backwards into the distance . . . beyond rescuers' reach;
a pair of horses who worked the towpath, drowning,
bound together, flailing against their cords,

a child-sized coffin, waterborne, when a corner of the cemetery,
"Precieux Sang," slid.

This happened long before I was born, yet my aunts swoon,
as if they might faint, and say I need to hear
the miracle of Maurice, who clung for life to his buckled porch,

a rocking chair still on it, aloft in the rapids—
when it hit the bridge and split. Somehow he climbed
to the top of the riprap and looking up, like Noah
from the flood, swore

he saw the eye of the storm pass over,
a momentary flare of sun, a blinding white—
the shape of a dove—

My aunts, blessing themselves, say,
"Mon Dieu, what Maurice saw
was the Holy Spirit come, here. Right here."

And fall to their knees,
kissing the ground, beneath their wash, unwavering.

Blackstone River Flood, Atlantic Mills, Manville

🖎 This 1927 storm, the flood of record until 1955 in the Blackstone
Valley, threw thousands out of work & homeless families into municipal
poor farms—heralding three decades of mill closures and economic
hard-times. Woonsocket was later named "America's Spunkiest City"
by *Look* and *Business Week* magazines.

World Heavyweight Champ Comes To Pawtucket

*"...notwithstanding the dark picture I have presented of the state of the
nation, I do not despair of this country." Frederick Douglass, July 5, 1852*

1911: The town newly strung with telephone lines,
prosperous, *in the black*
and in the streets,
new means of locomotion—a mile a minute!

Buzz in the air of a real celebrity, Jack Johnson "The Galveston
Giant," *heavyweight champion, first darky prizefighter*
coming here for the Fourth of July!
He'll drive his Stanley Steamer in our Grand Parade

ahead of the order of Hibernians, Knights of Columbus,
and the fife and drum corps!
Believe you me, that prizefighter, would never,
not ever, be seen

somewhere not free,
busted up, down-and-out,
out of gas or *in the red.*
Nope, a city's gotta be in the black for Jack to want the key.

He's Number One so you bet he wants to celebrate with us;
we've got the finest craftsmen, all materials
needed for war, a great river for freight . . .
So many of America's firsts!

Yup, *last* July Fourth,
Jack had Jeffries on the ropes for fifteen rounds—
"his fists fell like fireworks" they say,
(n' he sure riled those whites in Reno, mad as hornets n' still are)

❧ Jack Johnson was one of the few who dared to challenge the racial taboos of the early 1900s. After his defeat of Jim Jeffries he was America's villain. (Dan Bryan, American History USA)

First darky heavyweight champion of the world!
Newspapermen are warning the coloreds "don't be too proud,"
but we'll fly Stars & Stripes, colored streamers,
n' unfold our *Don't Tread On Me* pennant

cuz Jack Johnson's no average Negro,
he's no "Might-Be Negro Champion."
He's "THE Mister Champion Negro"
to his friends (Papa Jack to his ladies)

n' he's all hi-stylin' and gold pocket-watch
plays the viola, recites Shakespeare, speaks Italian,
brings his pretty white girlfriend (curves to match his car)
across state lines . . . that boy does what he pleases . . .

Jack knows a thing or two about battle
n' knows the manly arts
(we're all gentlemen here)—
his big gold smile opens doors.

Heck, we'll raise Pocahontas from the dead if he wants her,
cuz it's the nation's jubilee!
Emancipation changed everything 'n
now everybody's free.

June 25, 1910, Congress passed the White Slave Traffic Act, or the Mann Act, making it a crime to transport women across state lines "for the purpose of prostitution or debauchery, or for any other immoral purpose." Along with other moral purity movements of the period (which often did not distinguish between sexually active women and prostitutes) this had its roots in fears over the rapid changes industrialization had brought to American society: immigration, the changing role of women, and evolving social mores. It was ostensibly aimed at keeping innocent, immigrant girls from being lured into prostitution but really offered a way to criminalize consensual sexual activity, including premarital and extramarital relationships involving inter–state travel. The law was also used for racist purposes: Jack Johnson was prosecuted and convicted in 1913 for bringing a white girlfriend from Pittsburgh to Chicago, but the motivation for his arrest was public outrage over his marriages to white women. The Mann Act was born during the "white slavery" hysteria of the early 20th century. (pbs.org; www.history.com/this-day-in-history)

The Johnsons were booked on the *Titanic's* last voyage in 1912.
Shortly before sailing, they were denied passage.

Coffle

A train of slaves or animals fastened together, usually driven along
(Oxford dictionary)

On hills, the coffle makes poor time.
Time is money;
the slave drivers on their flanks
grow mean.

Bound together by rope,
moved over-land
from Charleston, to auction
in Natchez and New Orleans,

a young mother falls
out of line to lift her crying child;
like oxen under yoke,
the others fall back in.

She stumbles to the side with her boy
toward a stream,
where livestock (the other kind)
are let loose to drink.

A crack—she's on her knees.
Her throat swollen brown with dust,
the thirst she feels is under her skin,
in the soles of her feet

and it couldn't be helped.
Gun-barrels in sunlight
glint. She does not look; she looks away.
What does she see?

Slash marks
in the distance
on fields cleared by slaves,
scars on her wrists, re-bound

as her son turns away
to watch a cowbird . . .
fly round and round.

🪶 The slave trade was a vital part of R.I.'s economy, insuring cotton for textiles and sugar cane for rum-making. Many slaves were taken on R.I. ships between Africa, the Caribbean, and the South. An estimated 70–80% of North America's slave ships departed from Ocean State ports.

The Work

sinuous bodies
barefoot
back-breaking
picking
in dry fields
cotton in bloom
in baskets
babies
on the ground
sung to

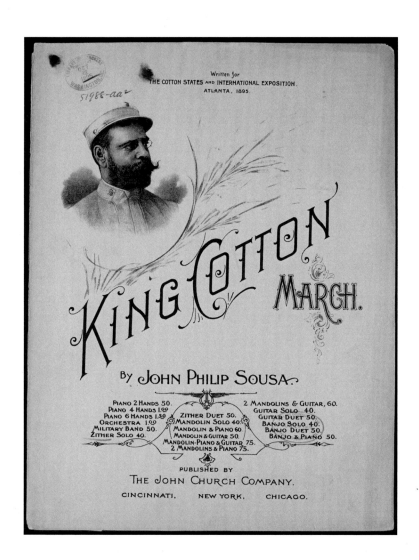

Written for
THE COTTON STATES AND INTERNATIONAL EXPOSITION.
ATLANTA, 1895.

KING COTTON MARCH.

BY JOHN PHILIP SOUSA

PIANO 2 HANDS .50.		2 MANDOLINS & GUITAR, .60.
PIANO 4 HANDS 1.00		GUITAR SOLO .40.
PIANO 6 HANDS 1.50	ZITHER DUET .50.	GUITAR DUET .50.
ORCHESTRA 1.00	MANDOLIN SOLO .40.	BANJO SOLO .40.
MILITARY BAND .50.	MANDOLIN & PIANO .60.	BANJO DUET .50.
ZITHER SOLO .40.	MANDOLIN & GUITAR .50.	BANJO & PIANO .50.
	MANDOLIN-PIANO & GUITAR .75.	
	2 MANDOLINS & PIANO .75.	

PUBLISHED BY

THE JOHN CHURCH COMPANY.

CINCINNATI, NEW YORK, CHICAGO.

Walt Whitman's Pants

O to be Whitman's pants!
When Whitman heard America singing, these are the pants
    it was singing in.

Laborers in trenches, digging canals and tunnels through moun-
tains, driving railroad spikes and wagon trains west,
    fifteen miles on a good day, wore them—

Kentucky Jean fabric, a cross of burlap and wool, from the Spring-
dale Factory in North Kingstown, Rhode Island, which also
    made blankets for the Union army,

along with fine flannels, and cassimeres
for the wives of industrialists and orators
    living in grand houses on a hill.

Whitman would sing the song of Mary Ellsworth, mill owner,
her dye house, cloth winders and presses, drying room and forty
    looms stretched with broadcloth, prepared for final weave.

The mill owner before her made field clothes for slave traders,
plantation owners, and sharecroppers, sold through
    the lucrative Negro Goods Trade.

    O to be Whitman's suspenders!

With leather ends and button loops called "galluses" to hold up
pomp and potential— thumbs hitched in the front, a confident
    snap, salute to an extra measure of character—

Big front pockets, watch pocket, welted rear pocket, notched
waistband, proud brass shank buttons for orators, laborers,
sons and brothers
    felled in ditches where the last road stopped.

Pvt. John N. Sharper, a printer by trade, enlisted in the 14th Rhode Island Heavy Artillery Regiment (Colored) on Oct. 30, 1863, later re-designated the 11th U.S. Colored Artillery. He was discharged at New Orleans on Sept. 11, 1865, for *phthisis pulmonalis*, another term for consumption or tuberculosis. He died on April 5, 1866.

Heavy Traffic

Dark water circles
ceaselessly.
Ships slip northward on
amnesia, full
of tobacco, cotton, denial

bound for enlightened Providence,
the mouth of the bay,
the jaws of the cotton mill,
the teeth of the carder and comber.

Dark water circles
ceaselessly.
Ships turn south
under the menace of storm clouds

filled with new, bright cloth, spools of thread, dry goods,
then call at Bristol
for silver, fine furniture, northern timber
for ships, barrels of rum and bread from South County

and on to Connecticut's wharves,
groaning with ivory—
tusks once carried by African slaves,
now bleached and milled

into hair combs, billiard balls, trinkets, objects d'art,
but most of all, in steamer trunks,
piano keys, silent.

Ivory in Connecticut

Start with middle C
and play it back thru time, thru
the juke, the clap, the hand, the cry
back through a century
of sheet music, cannons, "Yankee Doodle"
ragtime in living rooms—the middle-class pastime
before radio and gramophones
and talkies . . .

Play it down, down
through cakewalks and marches, burning
mobs, "coon songs," lynchings, "whites only"
peanut galleries and whites in blackface performing . . .

Play it 1-5-4 . . . and slow enough to feel the swing—
from Black to Negro to slave to ivory slave
over the bridge of sighs,
back to the clang of chains and iron . . .

Slaves carrying ivory for 45 keyboards from one tusk
for America's pleasure

Play it across oceans,
back to elephant-rich, central east Africa . . .
Tusks ripped from faces, bull elephants
dying through their sockets, sons torn
from mothers, men from their villages . . .

Ivory bound for 2 mills in Connecticut—
in Deep River and Ivoryton,
1500 workers *cut, bleached and polished*, milled each tusk
into hair combs and, mostly, piano keys—
a wafer-thin veneer—the perfect cover, the process perfected.

Find the key (in Latin, clavis),
show us the clavicles of slaves,
their *skeleton ribs* hoisting up tusks
by the ton, carried hundreds of miles to Zanzibar
on the Ivory Coast . . . bound for Connecticut.

Play it up . . . to 1954 . . . when the last ivory shipped.
   All told:
   Five Africans died for each tusk
   Thousands of tusks for American pianos

Turn the page if you want;
soulful player, I'm not singling you out,
nor your hands—weighed down
by silver and rings . . .
so lithe, flying across continents—dark, light,
   over those white keys let your fingers go . . . !

If I am singling you out,
it's to feel the pulse,
help find the key,
the skeleton key, the master key

Hold it till it hurts
and cuts,
till we feel its name
and say its name,
and cry/bleed/grieve
this one
thing that has cleaved
and cut

as ivory carried by an African slave
was cut into white keys
any one of us might have played,
starting brightly with middle C.

Ivory tusks stored in the Comstock, Cheney & Co. ivory safe, c. 1890

🐘 Through 1954, Deep River, CT was the largest importer of tusks anywhere in the world. One adult African elephant tusk of 75 lbs., properly milled, could yield the wafer-thin ivory veneers to cover the keys of 45 pianos. (CT history.org)

Comstock, Cheney employee cutting elephant tusk, c. 1900

Parting heads of piano keyboard with saw, c. 1920

ROSE LEAF RAG
A Ragtime Two Step

Scott Joplin (1907)

Lords Of The Loom, Lords Of The Lash

The beatings
The cleaning of flax and cotton
The carding engine
Boards with teeth moving in opposite directions
The pulling of cotton through teeth to comb it
Grooming the fibers for spinning into yarn
Stretching, twisting, spinning yarn into thread
Wound onto spools then unwound again to make the warp
The weaving of the cloth:
The bringing together of warp and weft
The weaving, the unweaving…the unweaving

The Civil War
Threatens good slave-grown southern cotton
and "Cotton Fever," the hunger for calico
and profit raging in the north—
For King Cotton, an unholy Union forms:
Planters and flesh-mongers of the south
Textile magnates of the north
Mill owners, flesh-mongers
The lords of the loom and the lords of the lash—
The engine of freight and cash
Feeding the country's insatiable need for
Printed cloth
Printed money...

Like a train
Like hounds in pursuit
This mill machine and field army
Once set in motion
Will never be stopped nor abolished
Vow the lords of the loom and the lords of the lash

Image of Army Officer Allen F. Cameron
"Let Soldiers In War, be Citizens In Peace"

Build Canals to Tame this Water . . .
A poem in two voices

    I.

First,

zero the origins, its name, in Algonquian:

    Kittacuck

meaning, great tidal river

    Sneachteconnet

meaning, rocks in or along the river

    Pawtuckett

meaning great falls or waterfall

    Wampanoag

meaning, People Of The First Light

Replace it with Blackstone, Rev. William

birthplace, England;

First white settler of Rhode Island and Boston

Build canals to tame this water. This Blackstone.

Erase the dark water,

the history it maps

Scratch

Narragansett   *Nipmuck*

Wampanoag   *Metacom*

Penacook   *Pequot*

Omit Woodland Tribes,

the "providential plague"

King Philip's War, as in,

the "First American Revolution"

the one the Americans lost

Silence
the tranquil tongues,
the patient farming rhythms.
Forget they taught us

to find food—
the way alewives and shad follow the stream
in spring and spawn;
how to bury a fish beneath the corn
to make it grow

Never forget though,
Be very careful for they are savages and watch us.
They go behind our back; they read our thoughts.

II.

We read your thoughts?
You fear us and care nothing for ours.
Did we let you starve?
Did we turn you to salt?

Your Roger Williams landed on our shores;
in the worst of winters, sheltered in our Sachem's hut.
Canonicus gave him land to found his sanctuary, Providence . . .
then a greater gift—*What Cheer, Netop!* Called him friend.

You tried to tame this water,
its tributaries and tribes.
You erased our totems, tribal lands,
all the birds and creatures bound to this place...
(not worth a red cent)
and would wash away all trace of ours, *injun* scent.

You scoff at our exchanging sacred wampum, as if
we are *paying*, as in, *money* . . . *Indian money*—
when we are saying, Thank You—the most precious gift—

because one life given so another's can continue, is sacred . . .
The quahog
gave its meat, its shell, its life
for ours to continue.
"Money won't do that. Money's not sacred."

Our totems became reasons to erase us.
You purged our myths, our moons,
broke the light into
shards and powders,
sacred wampum, into bits

so small, in-
significant, like us,
it had to exist
only in a place with room left over
for what was thrown away.

Postscript

And while I'm at it . . .

The pretty calico cloth can go too.
Erase the cloth, the cotton, Cotton Fever:
    flesh chained, flesh flayed
    flesh sold at auction
    of another "other," not native, not from here.

Then I'd like to stop,
intervene

on behalf of
the discarded, the sacked
the pillaged, red and black
and all colors in between

of every bird that flew, when
canals were built to tame this water.

Fresh Air Summer School, 1911 *(Don't Tread On Me)*

Their summer-school cots
placed side-by-side
become a tribal lodge.
Pale-faced, sickly,
doesn't stop them
leaping back and forth,
swinging clubs and tomahawks,

aiming bow and arrow
to pierce another red-skin's heart
and earn a stripe of war-paint,
the right to pass the peace pipe,
puff and talk about Tonto,
The Lone Ranger, his white horse,

and Jack Johnson, world heavyweight champ,
the first darky prizefighter!—
coming to Pawtucket for the Fourth Jubilee!
They puff and tell stories about The Galveston Giant
and wonder, who'll raise the battle flag?
Don't Tread On Me

The river Blackstone,
Kittacuck, Sneachteconnet
below them,
sunning like a lazy snake.

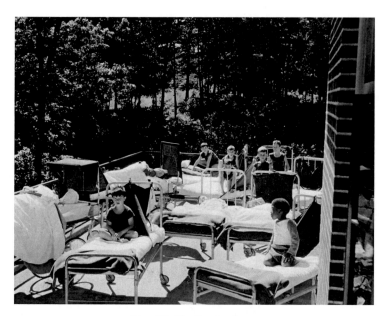

Burrillville-Sanitarium

Childrens' Pavillion, Sharon Sanatorium, Sharon, MA, c. 1942

The River, from Exchange Street Bridge.

Sunday Afternoon

Sunday strollers on the promenade,
the factories closed,
the river almost-blue, almost river-like.

The river-bank as it should be, elms
not yet sickened, green
thickness of willows.

Mallards strut, iridescent.
Sun-turtles shine in the muck,
an eel glides

luminous, past
boys fishing for pickerel
in the shallows.

Upstream, children build rafts of sticks
to watch them drift off,
break apart on the lip of Pawtucket falls.

A father and son skipping stones, circles
ripple, one into the other
as evening comes.

Tomorrow, the violence again.
The river goes crazy with color
the mills spew into the Blackstone . . .

It's said, you can tell what the mills are doing each day
by the color of the river.
Mustard, vermillion, lime-green, magenta on Thursdays . . .

Branding and burning the river—
heavy, heavy metals, dyes, varnishes, solvents, bleach
and a dark-red poison to kill the cotton seed bug—

a hot effluent slop
raging seaward, forty-eight miles
from Quinsigamond to Seekonk,

with all the waste that perverts this river,
all the measures destined for her soul.

Aggie's Angel

Still, he walks across my mind
though I hold out my hand and he's not there,
though his days at home were few, then none,
I remember this last half-year
and return to places no harm
could come.

He'd left
more starched handkerchiefs in his drawer
than used,
his lucky rabbit's foot,
deck of cards from Niagara Falls,
new Lincoln pennies under his chair,
his pocket comb, a strand of hair.
In his tiny closet,
two belts on a hook, idle neckties,
hornet wings inside his Sunday shoes.

Look, his gloves on the shelf!
I put one on
and clasp my other hand,
as we did
going places, everywhere
no harm could come.

Arrival Home

In the quieting air of afternoon, Aggie
colors—rainbows, a yellow sun,
    sky blue clouds (a giraffe takes a bite of one)
a pretty house without doors,
    smiles for windows,
a chimney's reassuring curl of smoke—

    Children standing hand-in-hand,
trees all around, apples
    falling everywhere.
A girl on tip-toes (or is she flying?)
    her hair, streaming,
reaches ever higher,
    higher than she ever has.

Afterword

꩜ I never anticipated writing a lyric history. This turn of mind surprised me, although I'd been told that deaths can do this—make you feel inseparable from the past. But the opposite happened first. With my parents' steep decline in 2010, I came unmoored, my compass spinning, my sense of belonging anywhere, blurred. I entered what would be a long season of amnesia. I stopped poetry— believing it added to my inner disarray— at least how I'd indulged in it. Ardently. Obsessively. (For example, I'd often written about Time abstractly, as an *object* of desire—to pursue, possess, feel its swirl . . . the chase took its toll). So to say, "I'm done," felt good. But could I be? My mode had always been to *speak* with poets, long gone or living . . . and those conversations are never finished.

the poets talk
constantly, I listen
back and forth between them

꩜ In the act of farewell, a discovery. Clearing out my parents' house after their deaths, I opened an illustrated history book of Pawtucket. Moved by an image of a "fresh-air" classroom, I wrote a poem. Then another. These became a pallet, and the pallet, a raft—to set out to explore a river, a region, my childhood home. So began a two-year, daily writing project with no idea what I was writing toward—pulled along by stories and the currents between them. No hunting, just gathering. Trusting poetry as an act of finding.

in fog I drift, watch
muskrats swim beside the banks,
feed on what grows there

❧ As a kid, I had nothing but time. There were fields and canals, a
dam house, a mill pond never far off, to muck in, skip stones, send a
letter in a bottle. Ideas of things rising from the water or falling from
the sky filled my head, for me alone to find. In mid-day heat and glare, a
vacant mill beckoned. I liked the cool emptiness, the smell of machine
oil and dampness. The way the light played across shards of glass and
broken tools, things that contained worlds. Every hour brought the
past straight in, although it never felt like the past.

geese fly overhead
homeward, I steer
from turbulence to quiet waters,
study subtle changes in the tide,
make entries in my log book

❧ The mill where my grandfather spent his life is being demolished.
It's slow work, outlasting the writing of this collection. The original
Howard & Bullough American Machine Company (later, H & B, then
Cumberland Engineering) towered and sprawled on fifty acres. Just one
section's facade remains—its splendid structural iron exposed. Perfectly
framed in my train window or visible while I drive down I-95 is a locked
chain-link fence. Within, are wooden beams stacked two stories high
and a mountain range of bricks awaiting a new beginning.

summer rain, unburied sky
and in the dust,
sun-struck cobwebs glisten

94

Demolition of the original Howard & Bullough Machine Co.,where
Pop-Pop spent much of his life.

Photo: M.A.M., June 2017

Time and work-worn boots found on demolition site.
Photo: M.A.M., June 2017

Acknowledgments

Thanks to Juliana and Will Anderson for conceiving their historical anthology and hosting events; to Historian Laureate Dr. Patrick T. Conley for his gift of words and books; to Tim McDuff of the Pawtucket Library Historical Research Center and Lori Anne DeCesare of Jesse M. Smith Memorial Library for research help. Thanks also to friends in the Ocean State Poets, and the Writers' Workshop at the William Joiner Institute for the Study of War and Social Consequences, now in its 30th year. Their humanity has shaped my work. And, above all, for Pete, who has shaped my life and whose story has become mine. Thank you for designing and creating this book with me.

Some of the poems first appeared in the following publications:

"Children Very Plenty," "Sunday Afternoon," "Lords of the Loom, Lords of the Lash"—*They Worked-We Write: Honoring the Lives of New England Workers During the American Industrial Revolution*, Eds. Juliana & Will Anderson (Ocean State Poets, 2016).

"Charity Begins At Home"—Telephone Man (Mayer, 2005).

"Fresh Air Summer School, 1911," "Kissing the Shuttle," and excerpt of "Positivity Posters" first appeared in the author's essay—"When R.I. Led the Fight Against Tuberculosis," *The Providence Journal* (March 20, 2016).

"Ivory in Connecticut"—Nominated for a Pushcart by The Origami Poems Project (2015). Originally written to perform with pianist Mark Taber, Aug. 2105.

"Kissing the Shuttle"; "Lords of the Loom . . ." read by the author on Good News Rhode Island (April 2016). www.youtube.com/watch?v=Ts8FOnQCA_w.

"Walt Whitman's Pants"—*Newport Life* (April, 2015).

Sources and Works Consulted

The following sources were used to inform the writing of the poems and supporting text. I've attempted to accurately depict sanatorium and factory life, natural events, as well as the harsh reality of local connections to slavery, and the displacement of native people. Efforts have been made to correctly reference indigenous language as is historically possible. I am grateful to all whose art and scholarship have helped to develop the cultural and historical background of *Kissing the Shuttle.* Steve Dunwell's exhaustive survey of textile mills was invaluable. In the main, two poets, Martha Collins and Faye George, served as models for how poetry can reenact and respond to historical and societal events. The conscience of this collection owes much to the lyric histories they have authored.

Poetry
Martha Collins, *White Papers,* E. Ochester, Ed. (U. Pittsburgh Press, 2012).
Faye George, *World of Hard Use* (WordTech Editions, 2015); *Voices of King Philip's War* (WordTech Editions, 2013).
Adrian Matejka, *The Big Smoke* (Penguin Books, 2013).
Carl Sandburg, *Harvest Poems, 1910-1960* (Marina Books, 1960).
Tom Sexton, *A Clock With No Hands* (Adastra Press, 2007).

Non-Fiction/History

A History of Rhode Island Working People, Eds. P. Buhle, S. Molloy, G. Sansbury, (URI Printing Services, 1983).

An Album of Rhode Island History, 1636-1986, Patrick T. Conley and The Rhode Island Publications Society (1986).

Connecticuthistory.org: "Ivory Cutting: The Rise and Decline of a Connecticut Industry."

Cotton and Race in the Making of America: The Human Costs of Economic Power, Gene Dattel, (Ivan R. Dee, 2009).

Journal Of The Outdoor Life, 1908, monthly issues, Trudeau Sanatorium, (Saranac Lake), NY.

On The Lake: Life and Love In A Distant Place, G.Wayne Miller, D. Bettencourt (Eagle Peak Media, 2009): www.onthelakemovie.com.

Pawtucket, Images of America series, 1996; E.J. Johnson, J.L.Wheaton, S.L.Reed.

"Stop Kissing and Steaming! Tuberculosis and the Occupational Health Movement in the Massachusetts and Lancashire Cotton Weaving Industries, 1870–1918," Janet Greenlees, *Urban History*, 2005 Aug; 32(2): 223–246.

The Historian (Burrillville Historical and Preservation Society); March, 1989; June, 1993. Burrillvillehistory.net.

The Run Of The Mill: A Pictorial Narrative of the Expansion, Dominion, Decline, and Enduring Impact of the New England Textile Industry; Text and original photographs by Steve Dunwell (David R. Godine Publisher, 1978).

"The End of Nowhere: The History of Tuberculosis in RI," Emma G. Sconyers, Senior Honors Project, May, 2012. digitalcommons.uri.edu

"The War On Tuberculosis," Peter Griswold, *The Rhode Island Historical Society Blog (Jan.6, 2012).* rihs.wordpress.com/tag/sanatorium/.

Notes About Particular Poems

The following poems draw upon specific sources, at times, staying close to the original. Both gratitude and apology is offered for poetic license I may have taken. Any omission is inadvertent.

Introduction: "the many-tongued neighborhoods…," "chemistry of turnip...": F. George, "Three-Decker," *World of Hard Use*, p.20; "where the farmer met the machine and the immigrant discovered America," S. Dunwell, *The Run Of The Mill...*, p. 112.

"Children Very Plenty": "a place very disagreeably suited...": Obidiah Brown quoted in S. Dunwell, *The Run Of The Mill...*, p. 15. Footnote on R.I. child labor: *A History of Rhode Island Working People*, P. Buhle, S. Molloy, G. Sansbury, p. 36.

"Kissing the Shuttle": "that spewed the lint that choked the lungs": F. George, "Mill," *World of Hard Use*, p. 16.

"The Superintendent Pins Up (More) Positivity Posters" shares a title with "Positivity Posters," Michael Casey, *Millrat* (Adastra Press, 1999), pp. 17, 45; some slogans designed by Bill Jones (from the web).

"The Nursery" (italicized text): Museum of American Bird Art, Mass Audubon exhibit, *"Nests, Eggs, Heartbreak & Beauty,"* Canton, MA, 2014.

"Searchlight": "quiet chimes in like clockwork", "trawling strange, waxed floors," and image of a welcoming house: Sarah Hannah, "Read The House," *Inflorescence* (Tupelo Press, 2007), p. 23.

"The New Creed": "labor multipliers," "strict behavioral control," "maximum production per worker" are attributed to Frederick Winslow Taylor, excerpted from S. Dunwell, *The Run of the Mill...*, pp. 147, 152. Footnote is from Wikipedia. "Gospel of Industry:" Psalm 141/Verse2 *Prayer for Safekeeping from Wickedness,* NKJV.

"The Mill Bell & The Clothesline": "patterns the lives that swing between...Saturday shift": indirectly quotes F. George, "Mill," p. 16; "many-tongued neighborhoods...," "chemistry of onion, cabbage, turnip," " clings to...horsehair plaster walls": "indirectly quotes "Triple-Decker," p. 20: both in *World of Hard Use*.

"Woonsocket: America's Spunkiest City": "but the cautious few," "the

100

danger about to descend," "floor-trembling...thunder": F. George, "The Pemberton Mill," *World of Hard Use*, p.17; the figure of Noah, "a biblical event," "drowned out every other sound": Tom Sexton, "The Great Flood of 1936," *A Clock With No Hands* (Adastra 2007), p. 25. Italics: *Providence Journal* 11/5/1927; cthulhulives.org.

"World Heavyweight Champ....": epigraph quotes Frederick Douglass's 1852 speech, Rochester, NY, "The Meaning of July Fourth for the Negro"; the terms, "Might-Be Negro Champion," "THE Mister Champion Negro": Adrian Matejka, *The Big Smoke* (Penguin Books, 2013). Jack Johnson's visit to Pawtucket is the author's invention.

"Heavy Traffic": "water circles ceaselessly," "under the menace of storm clouds": Rodney Lay, "Storm Clouds," *Chautaugua 8*, 2015.

"Ivory in Connecticut": Written and performed as a musical conversation with pianist Mark Taber, Aug. 2105. I am indebted to Martha Collins's *White Papers*, the second of her trilogy exploring U.S. racial history and white privilege. Borrowed phrases are italicized. Her poem [14], pp. 16-17, is the source of the piano motif and play on "middle C" in my first and final lines, and "skeleton key" word-play in stanza 11. Direct quotes: "45 keyboards from one tusk," stanza 5; "cut, bleached, polished," stanza 7; "cut into white keys...starting with middle C...," stanza 13. Indirect quotes: "five...for each tusk," stanza 9; "as ivory carried by an African slave," stanza 13.

"Lords of The Loom, Lords of the Lash" excerpts Charles Sumner: "an unholy union....": S. Dunwell, *Run Of The Mill...*, p. 103.

"Build Canals to Tame This Water...": "one life given... continue," and, "money's not sacred" from interview with Allen Hazard, wampum maker and member of the Narragansett Tribe, by Sarah Schumann, " Sacred Symbol" *(41′ N , Winter 2015)*, pp. 40-43. Dialogue between natives and Englishmen indirectly quotes "the way alewives...": F. George, *Voices Of King Philips War*; the phrase, *our first "providential" plague*; M. Collins, poem [20], *White Papers*, p. 27.

"Sunday Afternoon": title and last line reference Wallace Stevens's, "Sunday Morning." Epigraph is from a poster at Mass MoCA museum.

Author "Afterword" uses haibun, a Japanese poetic form combining diary and haiku, to lend the sense of a journey.

Image Source List

p. 2 "Mills On Blackstone River," from the collection of Gail Conley.

R.I. State Archives, Office of the Secretary of State
No known restrictions on use.
Frontispiece: "Pawtucket River and Falls -1855"
sos.ri.gov/virtualarchives/items/browse?tags=Pawtucket
p. 8 "Pawtucket Falls and the Blackstone River"
sos.ri.gov/virtualarchives/items/show/187.

Photographs of the National Child Labor Committee Collection
Library of Congress Prints and Photographs Division
Hine, Lewis Wickes, photographer. No known restrictions on use.
Front cover, p. 10 "A moment's glimpse of the outer world…"
loc.gov/pictures/item/ncl/20040062/pp/
p.10 "Spinners and doffers…" loc.gov/item/ncl2004001270/pp/
p.12 "Sadie Pfeiffer, 48 inches high…"
loc.gov/pictures/item/ncl2004001284/pp/
p. 15 "Girls at weaving machine…"
loc.gov/pictures/collection/nclc/item/ncl2004000242/pp/
p.12 "A Young Spooler in Roanoake, VA, Cotton Mill"
loc.gov/item/ncl2004002865/pp/
p. 59 "Noon Hour. Group of Workers at American Yarn Mfg., Pawtucket"
loc.gov/item/ncl2004001496/pp/

Other mill worker images. No known restrictions on use.
p. 17 "Young woman in the act of kissing the shuttle," p.13 "Carder breathing in cotton," historicipswich.org/2017/02/19/kiss-of-death/

New Deal Agencies: Public Works Administration
No known restrictions on use.
p. 87 "Burrillville-Sanitarium," National Archives Record Group 69N, livingnewdeal.org/projects/rhode-island-state sanitarium-main-building-burrillville-ri/

Other TB sanatorium images. No known restrictions on use.
p. 26 Wallum Lake children. Courtesy of G. Wayne Miller. Photo by State of R.I. employee. Long in the public domain.
p. 27 "Wallum cots on porch," p. 31-32 Newspaper images: "69 Take Friedman Cure," *Washington Post* (1877-1954) Apr 10, 1913; "Against Friedman Cure," *Boston Daily Globe* (1872-1922) Sept 5, 1913. Source: Pro-Quest Historical Newspapers. p. 39, "Wallum Lake Frolics A Success"; *The Northern Rhode Islander,* Jan. 9, 1941. p. 38, Patients enjoying buggy ride/variety show. Courtesy of The Jesse M. Smith Memorial Library archives, Harrisville, R.I.
p. 6 Childrens' Pavillion, Sharon (MA) Sanatorium, "Two girls with doll"; p. 87, "Boys on porch," Archives & Research Center, Trustees of Reservations. Gift from private collection.

Public health campaign images. No known restrictions on use.
p. 25 "For My Sake, Don't Spit," 1920; Lung and TB Association Emblems; p.57, 106; Christmas Seals: Univ. of VA Historical Collections of the Claude Moore Health Sciences Library. p. 25 Product ad from *J. of The Outdoor Life*, 1908, Trudeau Sanatorium.

Providence Public Library, R.I. Photograph Collection.
p. 63 "Blackstone River Flood, Atlantic Mills" No restrictions on use.
provlibdigital.org/solr-search?q=atlantic+mills+blackstone+river+flood

The Elizabeth J. Johnson Pawtucket History Research Center at the Pawtucket Public Library. No stated restrictions on use.
Front cover, p. 20 "Open-air schoolroom at the Summit St. School in Pawtucket, 1910"
p. 21 "Open-air classroom at Slater Jr. High School, 1920"

p. 21 "Pupils at the Meeting Street school were served hot meals at mid-morning and at noon"

p. 51 "Ladies punching time-cards in a time-clock, c. 1920"

p. 51 "Reproduction of City of Pawtucket flag, adopted 1974"

p. 59 "St. Jean Baptiste Day Parade, 1906, Pawtucket"

p. 60 "Illustration of a shoeshine boy and a paper boy"

p. 88 "The River, from Exchange Street Bridge, strolling couple, 1880's"

The Library of Congress Celebrates the Songs of America

p. 79 "Rose Leaf Rag," Scott Joplin (Joseph M. Daly Music Publishing, 1907), loc.gov/item/sousa.20028364; p. 71, "King Cotton March," John Philip Sousa (John Church Co.,1895), loc.gov/item/sousa.20028364; Composed for the Cotton States and International Exposition (1895, Atlanta) and dedicated to the people of Georgia.

Slave-trading and slavery images. No known restrictions on use.

p.69 "Coffle," cartouche from illustrated map, "Slave-trading routes 1810-1860," Lazlo Kubing. Source: Digital Scholarship Lab, U. Richmond, VA.

p. 70 "African American child and woman picking cotton in the South"; Vachon, John, photographer. Library of Congress; Look magazine photograph collection. http://loc.gov/pictures/resource/ppmsca.19948/

Photographs of Civil War soldiers. No known restrictions on use.

p. 81 U.S. Army Officer Allen F. Cameron, "Let Soldiers In War be Citizens In Peace," Library of Congress, National Union Catalog of Manuscript Collections, Rhode Island 11th U.S. Heavy Artillery (Colored) collection, 1853-1913.
loc.gov/coll/nucmc/2013CivilWar/04_RhodeIsland.html.

p. 73 Pvt. John N. Sharper, civilwartalk.com/threads/private-john-n-sharper-11th-u-s-colored-artillery.100188/#post-1271662.

Photographs of boxer Jack Johnson.

p. 65 Johnson in boxing gloves: Library of Congress Prints and Photographs Division. Photographic prints – 1910, Baine collection, Lot 10817.

p. 67 Driving car; On train with wife. From the web, in public domain.

Photographs of ivory milling. No known restrictions on use. Treasures of CT Libraries, Ivoryton Library Association Archives Collection, cslib.cdmhost.com/. E.D. Moore Collection.

p. 78 "Comstock, Cheney employee cutting elephant tusk, c. 1900": no. A2150 084278; "Photograph, parting heads of piano keyboard with saw...c. 1920": no. A2150 086067 3; p. 77, " Ivory tusks stored in the Comstock, Cheney & Co. ivory safe, c. 1890": no. A21500865461

Photographs taken by author

p. 50 "New World, Old World Bells, 1865" is a poster at Slater Mill.

p. 95 Mill demolition; p. 96, Boots found on demolition site.

TB Progress Note

Many people think of TB as a disease of the past, but a century later, TB remains an epidemic in much of the world. An estimated 9 million new cases a year cause the deaths of 1-1/2 million people, mostly in developing countries. Even in the United States, too many people still suffer from TB. It is preventable and curable, but this depends, as ever, on strong public health programs. In 2016, the U.S. continued to make slow progress, and at this current rate will not reach the goal of TB elimination in this century. (2016 Surveillance Report, Centers for Disease Control)

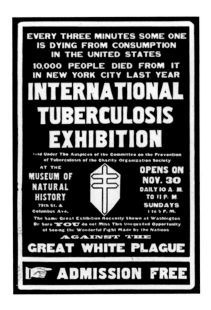

A free exhibit at the Museum of Natural History (NY). It is the only U.S. museum to ever have a curatorial department devoted to public health (albeit short-lived,1909-1922). Exhibits linked public health and education with society's progress.

Author Note

More than writing this book, I felt I was weaving it. In a tapestry or a society, each thread crosses over others. It's this weave that makes us strong, and able to call a place "home." I hope my book pleases and informs. I loved writing at the intersection of history and poetry. Both, an act of finding. Both land me somewhere unexpected. Both deepen the questions. If history tells us what the world was, science what the world is, can art show us what our feelings and obligations to that world *are*?

I care about what makes a healthier, fairer society, in which the most vulnerable can participate. As an occupational therapist, I'm attuned to elements which either enable or hinder us. The latter? Those who build walls, decree who is fit to belong, and erode hope. My hope lies in our ability to revisit our common history, and its mistakes and lessons, with an open heart. This, in no small measure, is the Rhode Island story.

The author (r) and friend Kathy Packer, age 4
Photo design by Diane West King

Mary Ann Mayer has three books of poetry, including *Salt & Altitudes* and *Telephone Man*. Her poems, essays, and translations have been widely published. Her honors include the GrubStreet Poetry Prize, a Massachusetts Cultural Council grant, Massachusetts Book Award and Pushcart nominations. In recent years, she has been short-listed for several awards, including the May Sarton New Hampshire Book Award. Mary Ann is an editor for *Crosswinds* poetry journal and volunteers with the Ocean State Poets, promoting poetry in under-served communities. She attended Boston University and Tufts, and had an occupational therapy practice for many years. She divides her time between Sharon, MA and Franconia, NH, where she keeps her dog-eared Nancy Drew books close by.